Follow the Money

A Citizen's Guide to Local Government

By Lynndee Kemmet

AMERICAN INSTITUTE *for* ECONOMIC RESEARCH
Great Barrington, MA

Follow the Money: A Citizen's Guide to Local Government
Economic Bulletin, Vol. L No. 10 October 2010

Published by:
American Institute for Economic Research
Economic Bulletin
250 Division Street
PO Box 1000
Great Barrington, MA 01230
888-528-1216
info@aier.org
www.aier.org

Economic Bulletin (ISSN 0424–2769) (USPS 167–360) is published once a month at Great Barrington, Massachusetts, by American Institute for Economic Research, a scientific and educational organization with no stockholders, chartered under Chapter 180 of the General Laws of Massachusetts. Periodical postage paid at Great Barrington, Massachusetts. Printed in the United States of America. Subscription: $59 per year. POSTMASTER: Send address changes to *Economic Bulletin*, American Institute for Economic Research, Great Barrington, Massachusetts 01230.

Book Design and Production: Jonathan Sylbert
Cover Design: Jessica Shiner

ISBN 13: 978-091361076-3
Printed in U.S.A.

Contents

1

Your Government, Your Money

THE RECESSION that hit the United States starting in late 2007 had a sobering effect on local governments and their citizens. The initial impact was a drastic reduction in revenues followed by drastic cuts in services. If there is a silver lining to the recessionary cloud, it is that these service-level reductions have reminded citizens of the huge role local government plays in their daily lives and of their need to pay heed to the financing and budgeting of their governments.

The issue of proximity of government to the people was central to a debate among the Founding Fathers over the proposed new Constitution. In simple terms, Anti-Federalists wanted government to be as close to the people as possible, which meant the greatest amount of power would rest with states and local governments. Federalists argued that America's initial form of government—the Articles of Confederation, under which states held most of the power—had been a failure because the central government was far too weak to be effective. They advocated for a more powerful central government.

The Federalists won the battle, creating the present two-tiered system consisting of the federal government and the states. Local government was not mentioned in the new Constitution. It was then, as now, completely under the control of states, existing only because states allowed it to exist and having only the powers granted to it by the states.

While some might interpret this to mean that local governments are powerless, the reality is that they are extremely powerful. States might tweak the powers and authority granted to counties, cities, towns, and villages. But no state has shown the will to make drastic changes in local structure and power. This is because local governments really are closest to the people and have shown tremendous skill in organizing their citizens to oppose state threats to local power.

Local government most impacts the daily lives of Americans. It provides police and fire protection, clears the roads in a snowstorm, and maintains the parks and swimming pools. It also keeps the water flowing and carries away the sewage, makes the decisions that determine the look and character of communities, provides social services, and educates the children.

But it's the level of government that receives the least attention from citizens.

The irony is that it's also the level people can most influence. The average citizen has easy access to local governing officials. The mayor can be found at council meetings, at city hall, even in the local coffee shop. On the other hand, even if the drive to the White House is a short haul, the odds are slim to nil that the average citizen will get a direct chat with the president. The closest most people will ever get to seeing their members of Congress in action is C-SPAN.

Money Makes the World Go Round

When it comes to government, citizens complain most about money: Government taxes them too much, spends too much, and wastes too much. Confronting the Internal Revenue Service and the federal government over money matters might be too big a challenge, but confronting local government is not. Yet, so few do it. Most citizens don't bother looking at the local municipal budget until the adoption of that budget is only weeks or days away—if then. Proposals to increase dog and cat license fees have been known to draw larger crowds to council meetings than discussions of the local budget.

One wonders why that is. Do citizens find budgeting too boring? Or is it that they simply don't understand the budgeting process and how to get involved in it? The answer is partly the first, but mostly the second. The budget process is far longer and consists of many more steps than most citizens realize. It's a months-long process. But if one thinks of fiscal distress as an illness—and many local governments suffer from it—the old saying regarding health aptly applies: "An ounce of prevention is worth a pound of cure." Waiting until budget adoption night to confront council members only breeds confrontation between local officials and citizens. That won't cure fiscal distress.

A How-to Guide on Following the Money

News reporters assigned a local government beat quickly learn that if they really want to know what's happening in a city, all they really have to do is "follow the money." Municipalities spend a lot. According to the U.S. Census Bureau, combined they spent nearly $1.6 trillion in 2008, the most recent year for which data is available. This is slightly more than they took in, as was the $1.7 trillion of expenditures of all the U.S. states combined. Where local money comes from and where it goes, makes for great news stories.

Unfortunately, the news industry, like so many others, is shrinking. There are fewer local newspapers and fewer staff reporters assigned to cover municipalities. The watchdog that kept track of the budget process for citizens is no longer always on the job. Citizens need to pick up the ball and start monitoring their own money because when it comes to local government, it is their money.

Monitoring the money is not as daunting as many might believe. This guide is a citizen's primer aimed at empowering citizens to work with elected officials and municipal staff in order to right what's wrong in local budgets or at least share the burden of budgetary decisions. The goal here is collaboration, not confrontation. The clash between citizen and local officials seen at the witching hour of budget adoption usually occurs because citizens came into the process at the last minute. They lack full information of how the budget went from A to Z, and local officials resent being questioned about budget decisions over which they've spent months agonizing.

Who's in Charge?

The Census Bureau counted approximately 89,400 local governments in 2010. These include general purpose governments, such as counties and cities, as well as special districts and school districts. The main focus of this book is on general purpose governments, particularly municipalities. But the guidance provided here is just as helpful in monitoring the budgets of special districts and school districts.

Most every local government is governed by some type of council or board. A board or council of five members is typical. But some counties, such as those in New York State, have legislatures with upwards of two dozen legislators.

School districts are normally governed by an elected board. So, too, are most special districts, but some are governed by a board appointed by a municipal council.

Fortunately, the Internet has made citizen involvement far easier than in decades past. Rare is the local government that doesn't have a website listing council and town board members with contact information. Most of these websites also post budget information, dates for budget meetings, and in some cases, a guide to the local government's budget process. Municipal websites also post information on key staff, and larger municipalities generally have a couple of staff people who play important roles in the budget process—the city manager and the budget director or finance officer.

Making Contact

What's true of most businesses is just as true with most governments. The important person in the organization is usually the secretary, which in local government means the city or town clerk. The clerk is the doorway to everything and everyone in town. Very often, this is an elected position, which means the person who holds it has a real interest in helping citizens and winning their favor. So the first step in following the money is getting to know the city clerk. If the clerk doesn't have the information you seek, he or she will get you to the person who does.

There are three ways to make contact—in person, by phone, and via e-mail. Large cities have full-time clerks. Most small towns do not. In really small towns, the clerk might only be at city hall a few hours a week. While e-mail is likely to be the easiest method for regular contact with the city clerk, it pays to make a personal visit to city hall early in the game. A face-to-face visit is the best way to establish a working relationship. Once that's done, if there is a city budget director or finance officer on staff, a working relationship with that person is next.

Monitoring Made Easy

This isn't municipal budgeting for dummies. This guide, written from the perspective of a local government reporter, provides insight that will help citizens track local government money in the same way that a reporter does. The difference is that citizens, because it's their money, can do more than monitor the budget activities of local officials. They can also play a decision-making role. This book tells them how.

There are two essential ways to approach budgeting. One is to see how much money is available and then figure out how to spend it. The other is to look at what services and programs must be provided and then figure out how to pay for them. Local governments often use a mix of these approaches.

The organization of this book starts with essential services. For that reason, once the local budget process is described, what comes next is discussion of how to play a role in deciding what programs and services need to be funded. That leads to the question: Where does the money come from? What follows is guidance in how to monitor local money as it comes in and goes out. Turning first to the budget process, it starts much earlier than most citizens realize.

2

The Budget Process

HALF OF U.S. local governments start their fiscal year July 1. That's one reason why stories about budgets abound in local media during the months of May and June. About another 25 percent start their fiscal year January 1, another 20 percent October 1, the remaining 5 percent at other times of the year. There also are some local governments that do multi-year budgeting, which means that the budget they adopt covers the next two or three years. This is usually only done in very small towns with very small budgets. It is not a very good practice for larger municipalities with a budget of several hundred thousand dollars or more, simply because such large amounts of money should be monitored more closely.

How early local governments start the budget process varies rather dramatically. A town of 500 citizens with a budget of $50,000 doesn't need to devote as much time to planning as a city of 500,000 with a $10 million budget.

The first red flag to citizens of a budgeting problem is if their city waits until the last minute to put some thought into the budget. On the other side of the coin, citizens who wait until that final budget hearing or the day of the budget vote to voice their views are of little help to the process. That budget probably has been in the works for months. Citizen pressure at the final hour usually results in much less dramatic change than what could have been made months before.

The failure of citizens to show much interest in the budget from the get-go often leaves local officials baffled about the sudden protest at the end. Most times, the fault is on both sides. Local officials tend to view the early stages of the budget process as an internal exercise performed during normal business hours. Citizens generally don't pay much attention to the budget until local media begin reporting on the final draft.

The optimum way to influence the budget is to get in the game at the start, not at the end.

A Long—and Sometimes Boring—Road

Many Americans were shocked when C-SPAN began televising Congress live. That's because people assumed the work of Congress took place on the House and Senate floors. But the cameras showed members of Congress standing at the podium giving their impassioned speeches mostly to an empty room. Those speeches make it into the *Congressional Record*, which is often the main motivation, but that's about it.

This isn't because everyone in Congress is out fishing. It's because they're off doing the real work of Congress, which gets done in the hallways, in offices, and in committee rooms. By the time legislation hits the floor of the House or the Senate, it's a bit too late to have much influence. It's the same with local government. Citizens who really want to influence the budget must get involved from the start. That start can be a good nine months or more before the budget actually shows up on a council agenda.

Budgeting can be boring. That's a fact. It helps explain why the media often ignore budget stories until the real impacts can be easily identified. But the real stories are the expenditure and revenue decisions made much earlier and often out of the media spotlight. Expenditure decisions say everything about what citizens and elected officials believe is important for the community. How they decide to raise the money to cover those expenditures hints at what they're willing to sacrifice to get what they want.

Advance Planning

In simple terms, a budget is a plan of what revenues a municipality expects to receive and on what it has decided to spend the money. Just as with any household, this can change. Revenues aren't always what the municipality hoped, and expenditures can be more than expected. Thousands of local governments across the U.S. learned about vanishing revenues when the recession hit in 2008. During less drastic times, all it takes is one bad winter for northern cities to learn how quickly snow removal and road repair costs can double.

There is no set time on when the budget process should begin. A mid-size city with a fiscal year beginning July 1 should probably be talking about that budget the previous autumn. A small town with the same calendar should be holding budget meetings the winter before. Even better is a budget process that looks beyond the next year and considers long-term financial goals.

A Citizen's Right

Experts generally view the budget process as having four stages—preparation, approval, implementation, and evaluation. For now, we're only concerned with the first two.

Keep in mind that it's your government and your budget. Most states have rather strict laws regarding open meetings and public access to government documents. This means that you can ask to see all the budget documents, and you can ask to sit in on early budget meetings. In larger municipalities with full-time staff, these meetings often are held during the workday. In small towns, the meetings are often in the evening. These early meetings are usually between council members and department heads. But a few citizen representatives should be allowed and welcomed.

To help citizens, many of the nation's larger cities publish a citizen's guide to the budget process on their websites. Many states also put together a citizen's guide for understanding local budgeting and finance that is available online or by request.

Capital versus Operating Budgets

Local governments can have a number of different budgets, but most lump everything into an operating budget and a capital budget. The operating budget addresses day-to-day operations and service delivery. The capital budget addresses big-ticket items and long-term projects, such as the purchase of a new fire truck or the construction of roads or government buildings.

Be sure to get involved in the process for all the budgets, not just one. The operating budget is the one on which the media most report. The capital budget is important because it often involves very large, long-term expenditures for which local governments must often go into debt.

Regardless of the type, all budgets should essentially follow five simple steps that lead up to adoption of that budget. If citizens offer their input during the first steps of the process—and if elected officials welcome that input—the budget process will be less confrontational at the end. More importantly, the resulting budget will more closely reflect the goals of the entire community.

Step 1: The Budget Request

Preparing a municipal budget begins with a request for budgets from the many departments within a municipality—police department, maintenance department, parks department, and highway department, to name a few. In large cities, that request usually comes from the budget director or finance officer. In a small town, it might come from the mayor or even the town clerk.

Very often when this initial request goes out, it has a few guidelines based on what the town expects the financial situation to be in the coming year. These guidelines can say such things as "Cut your department budget by X percent," or "We'd like to achieve goal Y this year so allocate funds toward that," or "Keep all budget increases within the rate of inflation."

Step 2: Departments Develop a Budget

Once a municipal department receives the budget request, it decides how much money it needs and how to get that money. The time and effort involved at this stage varies with the size of the municipality and of the department. In small towns, a department might be one employee. In large cities, a department might have multiple units, in which case, the managers of these units develop budgets and then bring those to the department head to formulate an overall department budget.

For citizens, this is the starting point. Look at the current year and past year budgets for each department. This will give a good idea of which ones are using the bulk of the city's money. These are the ones to watch. The largest expenditure in most every budget is employee costs. That's why departments with the most employees, such as police, usually spend the most.

The departmental level is where problems begin. If a department proposes to spend more than what the city planned to give it, that department has essentially three choices: Make cuts in that budget. Figure out how to get more revenue. Try to take money away from another department.

The first option could mean cuts in services. The second could mean increased taxes. The third could cause another department to lose funding. That could result either in a cut in services from the second department or a turf war. Such turf wars can quickly lead to budget gridlock.

A common sign of a turf war is a threat of dire consequences if services are cut. This tactic is most effective for police and fire departments. Most citizens fear reductions in police and fire protection, and these departments have been known to use this fear to their advantage. The problem is that if they win their battle to spend more than their budget allows, it means some other city department must take the hit—or residents pay more taxes.

Monitoring the budget at the department stage means that citizens will likely see tidal waves coming long before they hit. If citizens wait too long to address department budget shortfalls, the warring departments will have had months to develop their arguments for why they need the budget they've requested. And budget directors will have already developed their plan for raising additional revenue, which is often tax hikes.

Step 3: The Parts Make the Whole

The merger of all the department budgets into one creates the overall municipal budget. This is often called the executive budget because technically the city's executive presents it to the council and the people. At the federal level, the executive who presents the budget is the president. At the local level, it's normally the mayor. In practice, if a city is large enough to have a professional

Beware of "Fudged" Estimates

A tactic to watch for is that of playing with revenue estimates. The revenues that are in the upcoming budget are projections of what money will come into the local government. They are not guarantees, and they can be "fudged."

A simple way for departments to solve their unbalanced budgets early in the process is to increase their revenue projections. If a department sees that its proposed expenditures are higher than what it expects to get in revenues, it can simply take a more positive view and increase the estimate rather than cutting proposed expenditures. The danger is that down the road, if those revenues don't arrive, the department will be forced to make budget cuts in the middle of the fiscal year. Cuts that must be made quickly are often not as wise as those that had months of planning.

Don't be afraid to ask the basis of revenue estimates and to compare across years. If sales tax revenue is estimated to be $1 million in the coming fiscal year, but was only $800,000 last year, ask officials why they expect the increase.

city manager, this manager takes that budget to the legislative body, which can be the city council, town board, or county legislature. In a smaller local government, the mayor usually puts the budget document together for the rest of the council or board members.

Before this merged budget makes its way to the council and the public, the head of the process should meet with department heads to discuss their requests. These working sessions can involve department heads, the city finance director and/or city manager, and members of the local elected body. Often missing are citizens. These meetings are rarely widely promoted. But if a citizen asks to sit on the meeting, the answer should be "Yes." Under most state laws, if a quorum of council members attend a session, it must be advertised and open to the public.

Begin asking the hard questions. Dig into the details. If the budget shows a line item for salaries, ask how many salaries does that include and what are those positions. If a program costs $30,000, ask what it does and if the community really needs it. As with revenues, make comparisons. Have costs for a program increased dramatically from the year before? If so, ask why. Get behind the numbers to see what they mean.

Step 4: Going Public

Citizens and the media generally get in the game at this stage. But it's a tad late. The city's staff and elected officials have been working for months, so the budget document on which a vote is now scheduled is no surprise to them. It often is to citizens.

How detailed the budget document is that the public first sees varies greatly by municipality. Some have complete information for every department and program. Others are essentially a summary.

Most local governments, in fact, provide citizens with budget summaries that lack detail. Don't assume officials are being deceptive. Residents typically show little interest in budget specifics, and that has caused many governments to summarize documents under the belief it's what citizens want. Ask for more information with an attitude that says, "I'd like to participate in developing a good budget."

Going through the details can be cumbersome and confusing, which is one good reason why citizens shouldn't wait until the last minute. Neither should elected officials wait until the last minute to release the proposed budget.

There are no set rules on how far ahead of budget adoption day the proposed budget should be made available. But a municipality that releases it one week before the scheduled council vote clearly is not giving citizens adequate time for review.

Step 5: Public Hearings and Budget Adoption

Public hearings on the budget should be held at least a month, if not more, before a vote on the budget is scheduled. The whole idea of the hearing is to give citizens a chance to ask questions and make changes. A worst-case scenario is for a government to vote on the budget the moment the public hearing ends. If a government does this, the first budgetary reform that citizens promote ought to be changing this practice.

A good public forum should be well advertised in advance. Ideally, more than one public hearing should be scheduled so that citizens who can't make it to one, can make it to another. Town officials should allot plenty of time: several hours, not just one.

All the department heads should be on hand to answer questions about their department budgets. All the council members should be there as well.

The importance of the public hearing cannot be overemphasized. While some citizen representatives should have been involved in earlier steps of the budget process, the public hearing is the last chance for the mass of citizens to quiz local officials.

By the time of the public hearing, local officials have already invested a lot of time and effort into developing the budget. In their minds, they have already looked at the budget from every possible angle, have asked all the questions, and have come up with all possible answers. In other words, they are tired of the process and are ready to pass the budget and move on. But citizens need this chance to have their final say.

3 Where the Money Goes

RESIDENTS OF Bell, Calif., a small, mostly Latino town south of Los Angeles, were outraged when the story broke in the summer of 2010 about how much their local officials were getting paid.

The annual per capita income of Bell is a mere $24,800, with more than a quarter of the town's 38,000 residents living below the poverty level. But the city manager earned nearly $800,000, an amount far in excess of his counterparts in wealthier towns in the region. The city's police chief took home an annual premium salary of $457,000 and the assistant city manager nearly $400,000. City council members, for their part, paid themselves $100,000 annually for part-time work for which other cities the size of Bell normally pay about $400 a month.

Bell is but one example of excessive spending at the local government level. The residents of Bell, more than half of whom are foreign born, might have found asking questions of their local government particularly daunting. But getting expenditure information, including salaries for all city officials, is a citizen's right. Every state has laws requiring that such information be made public. Obtaining it should take nothing more than going to city hall and asking for it. If a municipality refuses to disclose such information, the starting place for help is the state attorney general's office.

Asking the Right Questions

Asking the wages of specific people borders on asking private questions. Asking questions about public positions is quite different. The question is not: "How much does John Doe make?" It is: "What is the budgeted salary for highway superintendent?" For comparison, the table below gives an idea of average monthly salaries in 15 of America's largest cities.

Had even a few residents of Bell gotten involved in the budget process, they would then have known before the budget was adopted how much of their tax money was slated to be spent on salaries. In fact, many U.S. cities pay salaries that seem extreme compared to what the average citizen makes. Monitor expenditures to avoid getting caught in the "Bell trap."

The More They Do, the More They Spend

Adjusted for inflation, the $1.6 trillion local governments spent in 2008 is roughly eight times what these governments spent in 1958. Government expenditures have increased at all three government levels because government is doing much more today than decades ago. The more services that governments provide, the more they need to spend. Local governments really are the frontline of service provision. When people need help, they usually turn to city hall. That doesn't mean city hall won't kick them up the ladder to state or federal offices. But municipal officials and staff are the most accessible government officials the average citizen can reach.

City Government Employment and Payroll—Largest Cities

Cities ranked by 2007 Population	*Full-time equivalent employment total (in thousands)*			*Average monthly earnings for full time employees (dollars)*		
	2000	*2006*	*2007*	*2000*	*2006*	*2007*
New York, NY	429.3	416.6	422.5	4,150	4,957	5,044
Los Angeles, CA	48.4	52.1	55.8	4,793	6,161	6,484
Chicago, IL	40.7	42.1	39.5	4,239	4,268	4,395
Houston, TX	24.9	20.9	21.5	3,037	3,633	3,753
Phoenix, AZ	12.7	14.7	16.0	4,024	4,951	7,278
Philadelphia, PA	30.0	30.0	30.2	3,637	4,390	4,618
San Antonio, TX	15.7	16.2	15.8	3,160	3,877	3,818
San Diego, CA	11.4	10.9	10.7	4,201	5,290	5,517
Dallas, TX	15.2	14.4	14.9	3,332	4,416	4,663
San Jose, CA	6.9	6.5	6.6	5,569	7,213	7,593
Detroit, MI	36.1	14.7	13.7	3,693	3,731	3,953
Honolulu, HI	9.1	9.1	8.6	3,435	4,318	4,575
Jacksonville, FL	9.7	9.8	10.3	3,815	4,377	4,248
Indianapolis, IN	12.0	16.1	15.9	3,115	3,536	3,617
San Francisco, CA	27.7	27.7	28.0	5,112	6,659	7,253

Source: U.S. Census Bureau.

Even the smallest town provides a range of services. Standard government functions, such as building inspection and police services, are only the beginning. Publicly financed libraries and parks address a town's quality of life. Economic development programs help provide for a town's future. Public welfare services help care for the young, the disabled, or the elderly.

The list of potential programs can go on and on, as the box outlining local government services on page18 illustrates. What all government programs have in common, whether local, state or federal, is that they require money. The taxpayers who provide this money have a right—and even an obligation—to know how it is being spent.

Expenditure Control = Budget Control

Controlling expenditures is the key to maintaining fiscal health unless citizens are willing to increase taxes on themselves to cover endlessly rising expenditures. Understanding expenditures and how to control them requires knowing what services are being provided, how much of those services are being provided, and which local government is in charge.

General purpose government—the government that typically operates out of city hall—is not the sole provider and overseer of local services. Education, which is the largest service in terms of scope and cost, is usually managed by a school board that is elected separately from the city council. Local spending on education is enormous, totaling $594 billion nationally, more than seven times the $77.6 billion spent locally on police services, one of the vital services provided by general purpose governments.

Many other services are provided by special districts rather than the general purpose government. In a large city, a separate mass transportation district board might oversee the city's bus and train service. This board might be elected or appointed. If elected, the board would be independent of the city council.

Gathering information on the money spent to provide local services begins with knowing what local government entity provides that service. To get complete budget information, citizens will need to visit the offices of the school board or transportation district board or whatever boards oversee special services. None of this is really as complicated as it seems. The city/town clerk should easily be able to answer questions regarding who has control over what local services.

Who is Footing the Bill?

Knowing who is paying for a service is as important as knowing who is providing it. If local money is being used, citizens can more easily decide to cut a service or to change how the service is being provided. If federal or state money pays for a service, cutting it or changing it might not be an option.

Suppose residents of city Alpha look through the police department budget and discover that 10 percent is spent on a special police training program. If the training program was created by the city and is paid for with local tax money, citizens are free to push for its elimination if they choose. But if the program was created through a state or federal initiative and is paid for by one of these

What Local Governments Do

Services provided by American municipalities include:

- Building/construction inspection and regulation
- Business/economic development programs
- Corrections
- Courts
- Education (K-12)
- Fire services
- Flood control (storm drain systems and soil erosion prevention)
- Health care services (health care clinics and hospitals, substance abuse programs, mental health programs, insect control)
- Housing and urban renewal programs
- Libraries
- Parks and recreation
- Planning and zoning
- Police
- Pollution abatement programs
- Public welfare (child welfare services, care and programs for seniors and the disabled, day care centers, meals on wheels or similar programs, after school programs). Many of these programs are provided by local non-profit organizations, but local governments help pay the costs.
- Sewage collection, treatment and disposal
- Transportation (road construction and maintenance, bus and train service)
- Water systems
- Other utilities (electric and gas)

other levels of government, eliminating it will do the local budget no good.

The picture gets a little more complicated if a program is financed through matching funds. Very often, states and the federal government pay part of the cost of local services and programs and require the municipality to pay the rest according to a specific matching formula. If Alpha's police training program costs $100,000 a year, for example, it might be that the city pays half the cost and the state or federal government matches the city's amount. This allows Alpha city to double the money it can spend. It also means that if the program is eliminated, half of the money saved goes back to the state or federal government. But Alpha city also does save its $50,000.

The Virtues of Summaries

Looking at the expenditure information in a budget can be a bit daunting if the budget is large and the list of expenditures long. The easiest way to get a handle on the expenditures of a general-purpose municipal government is to look first at the overall expenditure summary, then go into the details. Most local governments provide both revenue and expenditure summaries in the budget as well as summaries by department or service category. A good example of what is often found is the easy-to-read pie chart on page 20 produced by Hartford, Conn. It takes only a moment to see what the larger expenditures are in the city.

This initial summary gives a quick picture of what departments or services are the big spenders in the municipality. Compare current year expenditures to the past several years. This is an easy way to see if there are big increases or decreases in costs for a department or service. If so, ask why.

Big Spenders First

Start with the big spenders, and work down from there. Education is often the biggest expense for local governments that provide education services. County governments often have big health and social service expenses because that is the level of local government that normally runs hospitals and provides physical and mental health services. General-purpose municipal governments typically spend most on police and fire services—two services deemed critical to most residents. Small towns and villages with little crime might rely more on part-time police officers and volunteer firefighters, and direct more money toward libraries and parks.

Getting into the expenditure details means looking to see exactly on what money is spent. Is it being spent on salaries, equipment, or supplies? Then go deeper. If the budget for police services shows that $500,000 is being spent on salaries and benefits, how many police officers is that $500,000 buying? What is the cost of salaries and benefits for each of those positions? If the city spent $50,000 on supplies for general city administration, what was purchased? If half of that money went to purchase computers, what was the price per computer?

Most Americans are aware of the federal government purchasing items for outrageous prices, such as $100 hammers. Local governments make the same mistakes, sometimes simply because they lacked the staff with time to shop around. Maybe citizens can do the shopping around.

Digging into an entire budget can be consuming. West Palm Beach, Fla., for example, a city with a population of just under 100,000, produces a budget around 600 pages long. Few citizens have time for such detail. Starting with an overall summary and targeting the most costly budget items on down the line is one way to start understanding how taxpayer money is spent. The best approach might be digging into the budget details one department or program at a time, year by year.

City of Hartford, General Fund Expenditures
(adopted budget FY 2010-2011)

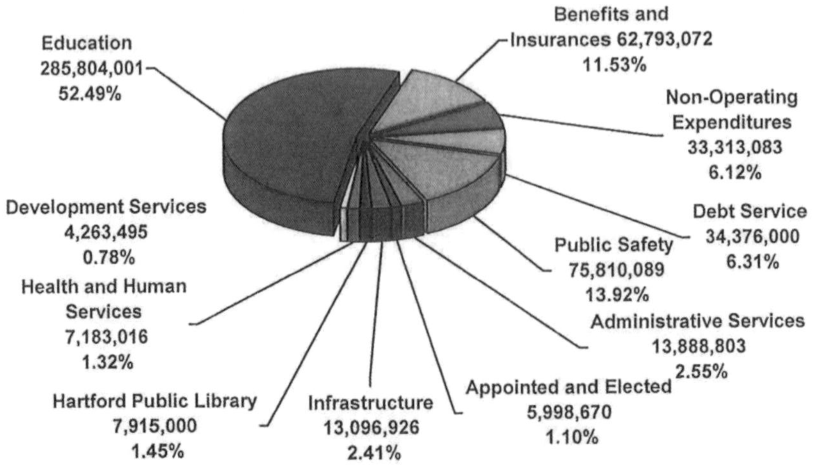

Courtesy of the city of Hartford.

Set Goals, Spend to Meet Them

Armed with an understanding of how local money is being spent, citizens can begin to ponder the question "How OUGHT money to be spent?" Government expenditures should be a reflection of the priorities and goals of citizens, whether in good times or bad. That's the ideal, but it's not always the case. Too often, the answer to the question of who gets the money is "those with the most political clout." This can be citizens if they get into the budget game early and remain active.

Goals pursued by citizens can be anything—parks near every citizen, the lowest crime rate in the state, the best social programs, or lower taxes. They reflect what citizens have decided are most important for their community. Rare is the community with enough money to meet all its goals. Most local communities must prioritize and decide which goals are the most important to fund.

Across-the-Board Changes

Deciding first on goals and then on how to pay for them may be the ideal way to determine expenditures. In reality, it's not what citizens are likely to find when they approach the budget process. Most local governments look at how much they spent the previous year and on what. They plan the next fiscal year from there. If municipal officials expect revenues to increase, often they simply increase the budget of each department. If they expect revenues to go down, they decrease budgets. Across-the-board cuts refer to situations when local officials expect revenues to be X percent less than in the previous year and tell all city departments to cut their budgets by X. Across-the-board cuts (and increases) may be a simple way to determine expenditures, but it's not always the best way.

Shaping the way a city or town spends its money is a process in itself, over and above the shaping of a single year's budget. Change won't come quickly. The process begins by asking questions about current expenditures and about how local money can be spent to create the community citizens really want.

Once goals are identified, a new raft of questions will require answers. Can the town afford to meet that goal? How should the town prioritize? Is there the political will to shift money from one service to another in order to achieve goals? What (and who) would be obstacles to change? How could this be overcome?

Out-of-Town Comparisons

Another question worth asking is whether there are cities of a similar size providing the same services and programs at a lower cost. Thanks to the Internet, comparison should not be too hard. The same town and city Web sites that post schedules for budget planning meetings often also post municipal budgets. Lacking that, these Web sites at least will post phone numbers of city and town clerks or other officials who can help you track down the information.

Be aware that a city with 10 full-time employees actually has as many staff as a city with 20 part-time employees. When comparing staff costs and the number of employees of different cities, look at full-time equivalent employees (FTE) as well as employee numbers.

Do We Need It?

Don't be afraid to ask if a particular program or service is necessary at all. Keep in mind that a competing claim from another government department doesn't have to be the sole reason for cutting an existing expenditure. Spending simply can be cut. A city or town with a full complement of government services might look great on paper. But the budget that supports these services could also create tax liabilities—particularly on property—that could be more than many current residents could bear. Because of this, over time, the very nature of a community could change.

4

Why Revenue Sources Matter

IN THE Census Bureau's most recent data, in 2008, local governments received a total of approximately $1.5 trillion in revenue. By comparison, in the same year, federal government revenue was about $2.7 trillion and revenue of all states combined was $1.6 trillion. And a portion of both federal and state revenue was passed along to local governments.

Revenues are important, not just because they finance those services and programs that create the sort of communities that citizens want. They also influence what programs and services cities provide. Citizens often don't realize that where the money comes from helps determine how their city acts.

If a city spends all its time trying to lure shopping malls, it might be because the bulk of the city's revenue comes from local sales taxes. If income taxes are a key source of revenue, city policies might cater to high-income residents. If a city is highly reliant on property taxes—as many are—city officials might prefer high-value housing developments to moderate or low-income housing. If citizens are anti-growth, yet town officials are the opposite, it may be that developer fees are a key revenue source.

How Secure Is That Source?

Citizens also need to know where the money comes from in order to see danger on the horizon. For both state and local governments, the Great Recession that began in 2008 created the steepest and longest decline in tax collections on record. Sales tax revenues plummeted as consumers stopped buying. Income taxes crashed as people lost jobs and income. Property tax revenues declined in municipalities hit by falling housing values and foreclosures. As the federal and state governments tightened their belts, they cut funding to local governments. Local governments cannot avoid all of the impacts of recession, but when looking at revenue sources, one important question to ask is this: How secure is that revenue source?

Perhaps the greatest mistake municipalities can make with regard to revenue security is over-reliance on one or two sources. Examples of this mistake abound, and one good one comes from the early 1990s, when local governments were also hit hard by the impacts of recession.

Moreno Valley's Bad Call

In the Southern California city of Moreno Valley, construction was rampant in the 1980s, mostly in housing developments that made it possible for the city population to increase by nearly 100,000 from 1980 to 1990—from 28,139 to 118,779. In the late 1980s, the city was adding about 4,000 new houses a year. It also was balancing its budget on developer fees. These fees—charged to developers for new construction that impacted city services—provided about half of Moreno Valley's revenues.

This was great during boom times. But when the recession hit, construction ground to a halt. Moreno Valley's budget crashed, going from a $16 million reserve in 1989 to a deficit within a few years. If citizens had been paying attention to the city's revenue sources in the 1980s, they might have seen the trouble coming. They would have also understood the city's pro-growth stance, because it was growth that fueled the budget.

Other cities make similar mistakes with other revenue sources. Cities in high tourism areas often have a great reliance on hotel bed taxes (transient occupancy taxes) and various forms of entertainment taxes. Such cities also tend to be big on building new hotels and resorts. But when economic downturns put a crimp on people's vacation plans, tourism-based revenue dries up. Some municipalities have been over-reliant on business taxes from one company or one industry and watched revenues shrink when hard times hit that business or industry. Detroit and the auto industry is a good example.

A Growing List of Sources

One hundred years ago, local governments got nearly all their money from property taxes. Fast forward to the 21st century and the list of revenue sources for many local governments has lengthened. Property taxes that once provided 50 percent or more of revenues for all local governments combined, are now only about 26 percent of the total revenue, according to recent Census data. Larger revenue sources for local governments are now funds received from the federal and state governments—accounting for 36-40 percent of total local revenues, depending on the year—and a broad category of "other sources" that now provides about 35 percent of total local revenues. Some cities even have income taxes; New York City is one of them. But this is not a tax widely available to municipalities.

This change is generally thought to be for the better. When assessing the strength of local government revenue sources, experts tend to look for both diversity and sustainability. Diversity means having a few good revenue sources rather than one or even two. Sustainability means these are sources that can weather economic storms and are likely to be around for years to come.

Start with the Big Stuff

For citizens who seek to become engaged in the budget process, the approach to understanding revenues is similar to that for understanding expenditures.

City of Hartford, General Fund Revenues
(adopted budget FY 2010-2011)

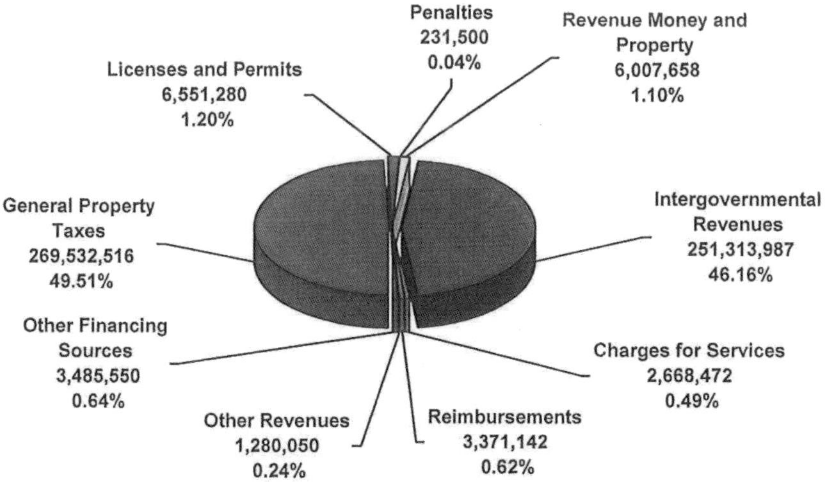

Courtesy of the city of Hartford.

Look first at the revenue summaries. As the example from Hartford on page 25 shows, like expenditure summaries, these can be easy to read. Find out what are the big sources of money. Are there one or two sources that comprise the bulk of the city's revenue? Then ask the deeper questions. How secure are those sources if the economy turns sour or business and residents leave town? As with expenditures, this initial look at revenues should include a comparison with past years. Is there a revenue source that accounted for 20 percent of revenues for five years and then rose to 40 percent one year or dropped to 10 percent? If so, ask town officials why.

If revenue sources are few and insecure, citizens might want to engage elected officials and city staff in discussions on broadening revenue sources. To do this, citizens need to know what revenue sources are available to local governments and what flexibility local governments have in using them. This varies dramatically by state.

State-Imposed Limits

Municipalities are creatures of their states. The powers they have—and this includes the power to tax—is given to them by their states. States set the rules on what revenue sources municipalities can tap, how much they can tax those sources, and how they must account for that money.

In Maine, the property tax accounts for about 60 percent of the total own-source revenue—the revenue raised by the local government itself—for local governments. On the other hand, in California, where there are limits on property tax rates because of Proposition 13, the percentage is only around 25 percent. Most states have a state department of finance or taxation, or similar state department, that can provide information on municipal taxing powers. In addition to guides about the budget process, many states also publish tax guides designed for local government officials. These can be great sources of information for citizens. The city or town clerk should know to which state department citizens can turn for this information.

5

Revenue Sources 101

BECAUSE OF the number of revenue sources and the variety by state, it's impossible to discuss every revenue source available to local governments. Even talking about them by category is challenging because the methods by which they are classified also varies. The U.S. Census Bureau, which collects a tremendous amount of data on state and local finances, tends to use four main categories of revenue—intergovernmental transfers, property taxes, sales taxes, and miscellaneous fees and charges. These are the same broad terms used by the Tax Policy Center, another good source of information on local taxation and revenue.

The percentage of revenue from each of the main four classes varies by year. The easiest way to quickly comprehend revenue sources is to place them in two groups—intergovernmental transfers and own source revenues. Intergovernmental transfers consist of money given to local governments from other governments. Generally, this is money from the federal government and the state. But sometimes this category also covers money from other local governments, such as from a county to a town. Own source revenue is money the local government raises on its own using whatever sources the state allows, such as property taxes, a local sales tax, or charges for business licenses or sewer services.

A local government itself ought to know what revenue sources are available to it. The table on page 28 gives an example of how much some major cities earn from the various main revenue sources. Another good source of this information is the state chapter of the National League of Cities. Such municipal associations exist to provide resources and information and can easily point citizens in the right direction.

City Governments—Revenue for Largest Cities, 2006
(In millions of dollars)

	General revenue							
		Intergovernmental	General revenue from own sources					
				Taxes		Current charges	Miscellaneous	
Cities ranked by 2006 population	Total		Total	Property	Sales and gross receipts		Total	Interest earnings
New York, NY	70,823	25,957	44,866	12,754	5,953	6,380	3,382	1,153
Los Angeles, CA	7,863	952	6,911	1,090	1,362	2,413	1,264	461
Chicago, IL	7,257	1,325	5,933	429	1,454	2,872	881	248
Houston, TX	3,119	550	2,569	781	664	808	269	153
Phoenix, AZ	2,903	1,115	1,788	261	692	581	184	137
Philadelphia, PA	5,809	2,478	3,332	394	225	698	184	105
San Antonio, TX	1,469	191	1,278	292	287	431	234	107
San Diego, CA	2,100	411	1,690	313	323	694	252	110
Dallas, TX	2,277	164	2,112	488	329	861	394	144
San Jose, CA	1,498	217	1,281	285	238	440	181	100
Honolulu, HI	1,337	197	1,140	591	114	284	50	29
Detroit, MI	2,132	694	1,439	309	218	452	119	47
Jacksonville, FL	1,829	323	1,506	365	371	383	379	207
Indianapolis, IN	3,014	646	2,367	1,486	47	506	224	94
San Francisco, CA	5,647	2,155	3,492	923	598	1,045	400	178

Source: U.S. Census Bureau

Intergovernmental Transfers

Local governments can use some money given to them by the federal and state governments as they choose, but this is not the bulk of money that comes as intergovernmental transfers. Most comes with strings and related costs.

Very often, federal and state officials use this transferred money to encourage local governments to do certain things. For example, to reduce water pollution, federal and state governments provide local governments with money to upgrade sewer systems, build new storm drains, and construct water treatment plants. To encourage local governments to address crime, governments up the ladder also will provide money for policing programs. And, of course, much money flows from the federal and state governments to local governments for education. Whatever their purpose, these funds are considered "earmarked funds," which means they can only be used for the purpose for which they were given.

Intergovernmental transfers also often come in the form of matching grants. To get the transfer, local governments must spend some of their own money. If the state gives our hypothetical Alpha city $50,000 to build a playground, the advantage of this giveaway looks much different if the city must match that by also putting $50,000 into the project. The state money is a good deal if residents had already decided that they wanted a playground and planned to spend $50,000 on the project. On the other hand, if Alpha city is in serious financial distress, and citizens feel the $50,000 should be spent on something else, then taking the state money will only force them to spend their $50,000 on something they cannot afford.

Grantsmanship

To get grant money, cities must apply for it. The process of applying for a federal or state grant can be amazingly time consuming. If a local government doesn't have someone on staff with the time and skill to write a grant application, then the cost of hiring an outside grant writer must be considered. Such writers can easily charge $100 an hour or more. Anyone who doesn't believe that the grant application process can be frustrating should take a look at some of the paperwork requirements for local governments seeking money under the federal government's Recovery Act economic stimulus program.

Such funds also often come with a deadline: The project the money funds must be completed by some specified time. If that doesn't happen, the federal or state government can decide to grant an extension. But it can also decide to take the money back.

A final issue that grant applicants must consider is what happens when the grant money is gone? If the federal or state money is being used to start a new local program, how will the city keep the program going when the grant money ends? Far too few local governments ask this question and discover down the road that they cannot keep programs without tapping a revenue source of their own, which often means raising taxes. Citizens need to ask: Is this a service or program we want badly enough that we will pay for it once the federal or state money runs out?

Own Source Revenues

Intergovernmental transfers, though large, only cover part of local government costs. Local governments must still raise the majority of money needed on their own. The revenue sources available to them are many and growing—too many to address them all here. But there are a few main sources that citizens are likely to encounter on the revenue side of the budget process.

Despite the grumbling of citizens and the focus of state governments on property tax limitations, the property tax remains the largest single source of own source revenue for local governments in most states. Another significant source is the sales tax, with fees, investments and miscellaneous taxes providing other own source income.

Property Tax

The Great Recession had a negative impact on homeownership and real estate values. But the property tax still remains one of the more secure revenue sources for local governments and a source they can easily tap when they need money. Rates are generally set by first figuring out how much money the municipality needs to cover its expenditures, then seeing how much money can be raised by all other revenue sources. Whatever gap exists between expenditures and available revenue from other sources is filled by the property tax. The rate is set to fill that gap. It is this flexibility in using the property tax to meet expenditure needs that makes it so popular with local governments.

Books have been written about the property tax, and there is far too much to say than can be addressed here. As with other revenue sources, it's wise to learn first what powers a state has granted local governments in the use of the property tax and to consider how economic downturns could impact this tax as a revenue source. And as with all taxes, consider the consequences of its overuse. Some taxation researchers argue that municipalities with property tax rates—and other tax rates for that matter—that are much higher than neighboring cities can find that, over time, citizens and businesses move next door.

Sales Taxes

Sales taxes are another important and traditional source of revenue for local governments. How important it is also varies by state. In most states, this is a shared tax, which means that it's split among various government levels. Generally, there is a state sales tax and a local sales tax that to the consumer looks like only one tax. New York State, for example, has a 4 percent state sales tax. But counties and municipalities can add a local sales tax of up to 3 percent. In this case, if a consumer pays 7 percent sales tax, 4 percent goes to the state and the remainder to whatever local governments added the local tax. Many states use a formula such as this.

Elsewhere, the state sets the sales tax rate, keeps a portion, and allocates a portion back to local governments based on some formula. The formula can be by population, in which more populous cities get a larger amount of the local government share of the sales tax. It also can be based on point of origin, which means the city where the taxed item was sold gets all the local share of the sales tax. Some states use a combination of these forms.

What can be taxed also varies by state. The best way to learn the formula in any one state is to check with that state's department of taxation.

Fees and Miscellaneous Taxes

This broad category has been growing over the years as local governments get more creative, and states grant them more taxing authority. The numerous revenue sources that fall in this category can include money from local traffic violations, court fees and fines, building permits, water and sewer services, business licenses, and dog licenses. In a local government budget, these will sometimes appear as one lump category listed as "charges and fees." Other times, the fees and charges will be broken down and listed one by one.

If a local government doesn't list in the budget each of the revenue sources that make up this category, it's a sure bet it at least knows what they are. Citizens should ask for a breakdown in order to really understand all the local government's revenue sources. If a local government doesn't know what's in this broad category, that's worrisome.

Although individually many of these fees contribute only a small portion to the total revenues of a municipal government, when taken together they add up. Cities in need of additional revenue might find that if they create two or three additional fees, those might raise enough to provide a service or keep a police officer on the beat. When looking at these revenue sources, ask what might happen to those sources if the economy changes or people simply change their behavior. If a city is making big money off of fees from a city-owned golf course, what if everyone stops playing golf and takes up tennis?

Special Districts

Because many municipalities make use of special assessment districts to provide services, it also pays to ask about these districts. The growth in the use of these districts is evident in the table below. In fact, while the number of local governments overall has decreased in the past 40 years—mostly because of school district consolidations—the number of special districts has escalated.

Special districts provide a single service to a particular geographic area. They have the power to assess, or tax, those who live within the district to

Number of Local Governmental Units

		Type of government				
	Total Units	*County*	*Municipal*	*Township and town*	*School district*	*Special district*
1962	91,186	3,043	18,000	17,142	34,678	18,323
1967	81,248	3,049	18,048	17,105	21,782	21,264
1972	78,218	3,044	18,517	16,991	15,781	23,885
1977	79,862	3,042	18,862	16,822	15,174	25,962
1982	81,780	3,041	19,076	16,734	14,851	28,078
1987	83,186	3,042	19,200	16,691	14,721	29,532
1992	84,955	3,043	19,279	16,656	14,422	31,555
1997	87,453	3,043	19,372	16,629	13,726	34,683
2002	87,525	3,034	19,429	16,504	13,506	35,052
2007	89,476	3,033	19,492	16,519	13,051	37,381

Source: U.S. Census Bureau.

pay the costs of the service. In most states, a special district can also borrow money by issuing bonds.

A benefit of special districts is that the service it provides is one less service the city's general fund must cover. A downside is that it's another tax on residents. Citizens need to know that special districts are an option for raising revenue to pay for services, but be aware that they can increase taxes and debt.

Investments

In recent years, the investment losses suffered by state and local governments have made much news. The pension funds held by state and local governments to pay retired public employees are what most citizens think of when they consider local government investments. These particularly took a loss in late 2008 and 2009 because of the stock market downturn. But local governments invest other money as well.

Any revenue that comes in and is not yet needed to pay expenditures can be invested. When residents pay their property tax bills, the revenue flows in, but that revenue might not be needed for six months. By being invested short-term, that property tax money is earning some income rather than just sitting around.

The income earned from investments is listed in local budgets under revenues. Not often listed in the budget is exactly how much is invested and where. That's what citizens need to ask. Many local governments pool their funds with other state and local governments into government investment pools that are managed by private investment firms. For citizens, the key is to know how much is invested and where and who is managing the money.

6

Budget Monitoring Made Easy

KNOWING WHERE the money is spent and where it comes from is only part of the overall budget process. Just as important is making sure that the budget is on track throughout the fiscal year. Budget monitoring is vital because the sooner you notice fiscal problems, the easier they are to cure.

The first two stages of budgeting—preparation and approval—are complete once the final budget is adopted by the local council or board. The last two stages are implementation and evaluation.

Implementation is nothing other than putting the budget in action—spending the money and collecting the revenue. It's basically the role of municipal staff.

Evaluation involves asking not only if the budget is on target, but also if it is meeting community goals. If the answer is no to either of these questions, citizens should start thinking about potential changes for the next fiscal year. Evaluation should be ongoing. If citizens and local officials evaluate the current year budget at the same time that they are developing the next year budget, then that next year budget will be far better.

Estimated versus Actual

Monitoring a local government budget is a lot less complicated than it might seem. It's much the same as monitoring a household budget, and both entities often face the same problems. Revenues (income) and expenditures are not always what local governments and households hoped. In governmental terms, this means there is a difference between actual revenues and/or expenditures and estimated revenues and expenditures.

Municipalities, like households, estimate that a certain amount of income will come in throughout the year. But a job layoff can mean lost income for a household, and an economic downturn can mean lost revenue for a city, as so many experienced in the recent recession. Unanticipated costs also can emerge. A sudden illness can add greatly to a household's costs just as a tropical storm can wreak havoc on a coastal city by leaving massive clean-up costs behind.

A household can't always prevent the job layoff or the onset of illness, and a city can't control the national economy or the weather. In a perfect world, both the household and the city would have a rainy day fund, which is money set aside to cover the unexpected. In the real world, few municipalities have an adequate reserve fund, if they have one at all—even though some states require them to do so.

Absent adequate reserves to ride out a fiscal storm, the next best thing is for citizens to monitor the budget for early signs of trouble. Most municipalities produce monthly or quarterly budget reports. Some very large cities create weekly reports. These reports should track expenditures going out and revenues coming in each week, month, or quarter. Very few citizens ask for these reports, but they should. If a local government doesn't produce one, be worried. These reports show whether actual revenues coming in and expenditures going out match what the budget predicted.

What's Behind the Estimate?

There are many reasons why estimated and actual revenues and expenditures can fail to match. But the key question citizens should ask is what's behind the estimates? Sometimes the estimated revenues and expenditures put in the budget are unrealistic. Our Alpha city, for example, might assume that because sales tax revenue was $500,000 last year, that it will again be at least $500,000 this fiscal year. But what if sales tax revenue the past several years was consistently $300,000 each year? Why is a dramatic increase in sales tax revenue expected to continue this year?

Often cities base revenue projections on what was received the previous year without considering that the previous year might have been an anomaly. It's best to base projections on the last several years, not just the past year or two. The same can be said of expenditures. Just because gas prices remained stable for two years doesn't mean they will for a third. Citizens might be surprised at how much municipalities spend on fuel, especially those with many police cars out on patrol. It's best to allocate money for the unexpected, and if it doesn't happen, then that's saved money that can be dropped into the rainy day fund.

Another problem with estimates is that they are often based on current economic conditions. But economic conditions can change. In the recent recession, income tax revenues dropped and sales tax revenues declined. Even the relatively stable property tax took a hit. During times of rapid inflation, on the other hand, local government expenditures can rise beyond estimates. Keeping an eye on broader economic conditions is part of budget monitoring.

Watch the Governments Above

Municipalities aren't the only ones with budgets that can go awry. Federal and state governments often suffer the same fate. When they get into fiscal trouble, they are much less generous in providing funds to local governments. This is particularly true of state governments. If they are in financial trouble, local governments face a real possibility of seeing a cut in intergovernmental funds. This could mean that money to repair a road disappears along with money to support a special community policing program. Additional funding for education programs can also disappear.

No matter what the source, if the actual revenue coming in throughout the year is less than what was estimated, then the expenditure side of the budget will have to be adjusted. If actual expenditures turn out to be higher than expected mid-way through the fiscal year, local governments can start cutting costs or hope that revenues will be higher than estimated. Revenues can come in high, but it's rare. This is where that rainy day fund comes in handy.

Expect the Unexpected

Much can happen in the course of a fiscal year that is beyond the control of municipalities. Local officials and citizens must simply expect the unexpected and think ahead about how to address disaster. That disaster can be recession, inflation, or century-old water mains that finally give way.

The budget is a plan, not a law. Citizens tend to step out of the budget process once the budget is adopted. As a result, they are not in the loop when changes appear partway through the fiscal year.

Not all mismatches between estimated and actual revenues and expenditures are bad. Revenues can be higher than expected, and savings can turn up. What if several employees quit and aren't replaced for weeks or even months? The result is a rather large savings in salary and benefit costs. There are many potential uses for this money—increasing services or programs, reducing taxes, or adding to the rainy day fund. Staying on top of the budget as it unfolds gives citizens the chance to play a role in redirecting saved funds.

The General Fund and Then Some...

Monitoring the budget requires a bit of understanding of the multiple funds used by local governments. When times are tough and local governments run out of money, nine times out of ten, it is the general fund that has gone broke. Citizens can get confused when elected officials claim the budget is in the red, while budget documents show funds flush with cash.

When most people talk about the local budget, they are talking about the general fund. The general fund is the basic operating fund for a local government out of which it covers day-to-day costs for the administration and provision of services. But local governments actually have a number of funds. The larger the municipality, the greater the number of funds it is likely to have.

There is really no end to the list of funds one might find in a municipal budget—from big capital funds to fire service funds to small cemetery and sidewalk funds. It's impossible to discuss them all here. But citizens ought to know they exist and track the money in them because mismanaging them can get a local government in a bit of hot water.

The easiest way for citizens to understand all the different funds they are likely to see in the budget is to know that the source of revenue plays a big role in determining the funds local governments create. Much of the money that the federal and state governments give to local governments can only be used for specific purposes. If a local government receives federal money for road improvements or to upgrade a sewer system, it can only use the money for those purposes. The right thing to do is to create a fund just for that money and put it in there until it's needed.

Capital Funds for the Big Items

In addition to the general fund, most every local government has a capital fund. These often have large amounts of money. That's because they cover the big money projects, such as buying fire trucks, constructing new offices, or building water or sewage treatment plants. The expenditures for these budget items are often called capital outlays. In small municipalities, there may be one capital fund from which all capital outlays are paid. Larger municipalities often have several different capital funds. The table from the Census Bureau below gives a good picture of the many types of large expenditures municipalities cover by creating capital funds. As with operating budgets, it shows that educational needs top the list for capital outlays.

The large sums of money in capital funds are collected over a course of years and include the local government's own money as well as money from federal and state sources. The funds also include a lot of borrowed money. Most of the municipal bonds sold by municipalities are used to raise money for these large capital outlays. This is necessary. Without it, communities would not have new roads, schools, hospitals, or sewage treatment plants.

Debt, however, can get out of hand. Census data puts total local government debt at more than $1.5 trillion. Total municipal debt 20 years earlier was about $453 billion—or $847 billion adjusted for inflation, approximately half of what it is today. The cost of servicing that debt, both in principal and interest, is a drain on local finances. How much debt a city is carrying, as well as its annual

Local Government Capital Outlays
(in millions of dollars, except percent)

	1990	*1995*	*2000*	*2005*
Total	77,578	93,611	140,830	183,119
Annual percent change	4.5	10.6	8.4	2.3
By function:				
Education	18,744	29,858	46,890	57,147
Elementary and secondary	17,669	28,402	44,629	54,068
Higher education	1,076	1,456	2,261	3,079
Highways	9,017	10,874	14,789	18,066
Health and hospitals	2,316	2,481	3,274	4,433
Natural resources	952	935	1,589	1,873
Housing	3,878	4,340	5,324	7,542
Air transportation	3,095	3,446	6,156	8,712
Water transportation	722	877	1,308	1,231
Sewerage	8,023	8,040	9,690	13,685
Parks and recreation	3,276	3,435	5,872	7,221
Utilities	13,996	16,801	20,615	30,560
Other	13,559	16,715	25,323	32,650

Source: U.S. Census Bureau.

costs to service it, should be listed in the expenditure side of the budget.

Fund Borrowing

Municipalities do sometimes borrow from funds with cash to cover shortfalls in other funds. The money may be separate on the books, but depending on state rules, it can sometimes be combined into one checking account. Mixing of fund money, if allowed, is a temporary situation. The normal practice is to keep funds separate. If the general fund is broke, the general fund is broke. Money from other funds cannot be used to cover general fund shortages.

In some states, it's possible to shift costs from the general fund to one of these other funds, if state rules allow. This can even include staff salaries. As an example, redevelopment funds are used by many cities for economic development projects. A city can hire an economic development director and put that person in charge of all redevelopment projects. This director's salary or a portion of it could be paid through the redevelopment fund, saving the general fund that salary cost.

7

Cost Cutting

LOCAL GOVERNMENTS, like many households, are always looking for a less expensive way to get the job done. Over the years, a variety of methods have evolved that aim to help local governments cut costs. Two more widely used ones are collaboration and outsourcing.

Collaboration

There was a time, not so long ago, when many government researchers promoted the merging of local governments as a way to increase efficiency and cut costs. Savings would result from eliminating multiple administrative overheads, such as going from two police chiefs down to one. Such mergers have occurred, but they are few. Citizens might complain about their local government. Try eliminating it, and they become its biggest defenders.

An approach more likely to have success is collaboration, in which two or more local governments join forces to provide services and purchase equipment and supplies. School districts have led in this, especially in purchasing supplies at bulk prices and then dividing them among districts.

Collaboration to provide shared services is increasing among local governments of all sizes in many forms: two towns sharing in the cost of hiring ambulance services, several towns buying an expensive dump truck together, one town paying to use another town's emergency dispatch center, or several towns building a shared sewage treatment plant.

But the road to successful collaboration is not always smooth. Negotiations between municipalities can turn unfriendly, and most any collaboration will affect someone in a negative way, whether real or just perceived. Employees in one municipality might face lost jobs if another municipality takes over service provision or some staff person will feel that his or her turf is threatened by the collaboration. Nevertheless, collaboration can be a useful method for reducing the costs of services without reducing the quality or level of service.

Outsourcing

As the name implies, outsourcing refers to having an entity outside of the municipality provide a service. This outside entity can be a private individual, a private company, a non-profit organization, or even another local government, in which case it is also a form of collaboration.

Municipalities typically hire private companies to pick up the garbage, collect taxes, and even provide ambulance service. They also hire non-profit organizations to provide social services such as meal programs for seniors or shelters for the homeless.

The benefit most cited is that costs are lower because as firms compete to provide the service, they keep their bids low. There are also efficiencies of scale: Firms can spread their overhead costs around to multiple municipalities with which they have contracts.

Besides cost savings, there are other reasons why outsourcing can be a good option. Municipalities gain access to expertise not available on the municipality's current staff. They gain access to better equipment and technology without having to buy it. Outsourcing also makes it possible to gain quick access to temporary, additional staff when needed. There can also be risks to some service delivery, and outsourcing places these risks on someone else.

Mixed Results

There are both pros and cons to outsourcing. For every study that claims that it saves local governments money, there is another that argues the opposite. The truth is that sometimes outsourcing makes sense, and sometimes it doesn't. Some local governments have outsourced services and saved money without a reduction in service quality. Others have outsourced services only to discover that the quality of service declined dramatically, that actual costs turned out to be higher than when the city itself provided the service, and that much public money was misused.

In reality, outsourcing is widely used and growing. Elected officials and citizens can have more positive results with outsourcing if they consider some things ahead of time. Number one is that the outsider providing a service might be private, but it is receiving public funds. Public officials and citizens have the right to ask questions and monitor the money, even when it goes out the door of city hall and into private hands.

Is the Contract Process Competitive?

By law, local governments must put contracts out for a bid that allows multiple businesses or organizations to apply. Theoretically, governments should take the lowest bid. In reality, they also consider such things as the ability of bidding companies to provide the service. A one-person business can bid on a city contract for trash collection, but can that sole proprietor really collect all the garbage?

If there is no competition among firms for the contract to provide a public service, then the argument that competition keeps costs down doesn't hold. For there to be competition, there must be more than one company in town qualified to provide a service. In some cities, even in large cities, competition for contracts might not be possible. In such a case, the sole qualified provider can still get the contract, but citizens and elected officials should always work to encourage other potential companies to apply.

If a city contracts with the same company year after year for a service delivery, question whether too close a relationship has developed between the city and the company. Do other companies really have a fair chance of taking the contract away from the current company? Think like a reporter. Find out if other qualified companies have applied for the city contract with no success, and ask why.

A Question of Quality

The cost savings from outsourcing might not always be a good thing. Get the details. It may be that the private company's employees receive low wages and poor benefits. Some municipalities actually require that their contractors pay employees wages that are on par with what the municipality's employees earn.

Private firms might also do the job more cheaply by cutting corners. A city ambulance service might have as its goal a 10-minute response time, and to achieve this, keep enough staff and equipment on the job at all times to reach anywhere in the city in 10 minutes. A private firm might set a response time at 15 minutes, allowing it to reduce the number of ambulances covering the city territory by one and having the remaining ambulances cover more ground.

Monitoring the Providers

Surprisingly, municipalities appear to be terribly lax when it comes to monitoring outsiders who are providing services to citizens. Although 95 percent of governments reported doing some contracting, according to a recent survey by the International City/County Management Association (ICMA), less than half reported doing any monitoring. Cost was monitored the most, and that was only done by 40 percent of the governments that responded.

Outside entities providing a municipal service should provide a budget just as any municipal department must do that gives details on how the city's money is being spent. Don't settle for a budget that says X number of employees will be working to provide service to the city. It's meaningless. The real question is how many hours those employees are dedicated to providing services to the city.

Most governments, once they contract out a service, leave it to the private firm to deal with citizen complaints. In that same ICMA survey, only 11 percent of local governments reported that they handle complaints about service delivery. This raises issues of accountability. Before the contract is signed, citizens should know who will handle complaints and what their local government can do if they are unhappy with the quality of service. Can the contract be nullified? Are there penalties for poor service provision?

Hidden Costs

Contracting isn't a free service. There are costs in terms of employee time putting together contract documents, reviewing incoming bids, discussing them, and monitoring contracts. These are often referred to as the transaction costs. Legal fees alone can really add up as no contract should be signed without thorough review by a city attorney. And, if things go wrong, that attorney will make even more money because city attorney fees run well over $100 an hour. But outsourcing can be successful, if citizens and elected officials cover all the bases before the contract is signed.

8

The Politics of Budgeting

ALTHOUGH MUNICIPAL budget documents can be hundreds of pages long, when it comes down to it, budgeting involves only two things—revenues and expenditures. It's not as complicated as citizens think or city officials might make it seem.

It's a simple process. Start by deciding what services the municipality should provide. Figure out the most affordable way to pay for those services. Look at available revenue sources, and decide how to use them. Then, on a monthly or quarterly basis, monitor the actual costs of those services and the income coming in to pay for them.

The biggest challenge is actually political. Municipalities aren't households where the parents can make all the decisions. They are communities of people with different needs, different wants, and different visions of what the community should be. The struggle for elected officials is to balance these differences. Citizens who opt to insert themselves into the budget process will face this same struggle.

Local Control Matters

Politics can be a nasty game. If anything discourages citizens from remaining involved in the budget process, it is likely to be the politics. But citizens must become active players in the local budget process because the stakes are high. Local government is the foundation of the U.S. federal system. If local governments fail, the decentralization that is an integral part of the federal system will be in jeopardy.

One could argue that local governments will never fail because the federal government will ensure that local services continue by passing down money if absolutely necessary. That's what happened during the recent recession through the National Recovery Act, which provided additional funding for local services. The increasing role of federal and state governments in providing financial support to local governments is not necessarily good. As the saying goes, "control follows money." If the federal or state government is paying the bill, it has the control.

It Takes Two to Collaborate

Fiscally healthy local governments are the key to maintaining local power. Thomas Jefferson had it right in arguing that political and economic strength at the bottom would result in a healthy nation overall. It is at the local level that citizens can be most engaged with their governments. At the heart of the Anti-Federalist argument in support of local government two centuries ago was the belief that when government is distant from the people, the people soon become disengaged from the political process. Once this happens, democracy fades.

Citizens, working with local elected officials and staff, have the best chance of strengthening local government by righting what's wrong in local finance. Collaboration, not confrontation, will result in fiscally healthy, independent municipalities.

Some citizens will encounter opposition to their involvement in the budget process from elected officials or municipal staff. Most likely, this will show up in an unwillingness to share information or in an attitude that citizen queries are too time-consuming and troublesome. Although citizens should seek to resolve such internal battles at the local level, when all else fails, the state and outsiders can be helpful.

Help from High Places

The best help for citizens facing opposition to their involvement is often the state. One top elected official at the state level is the state attorney general. The attorney general's office is often the state office most willing to help citizens, especially if local officials may have engaged in wrongdoing by mismanaging public funds or simply not providing citizens with public budget information and informing them of budget meetings.

Most states also have some sort of department of finance and taxation, which, in addition to dealing with state taxation and finance, oversees local taxation and finance. At the very least, these state departments will know where to point citizens who have questions about local finance. Members of Congress also have local offices with staff whose sole job is helping constituents. Federal elected officials are not always willing to insert themselves into local affairs, but their staff can point citizens toward state officials who will.

When it comes to turning to the state for help, keep in mind that states have also faced severe budget problems that have reduced staff numbers. Don't assume state staff will respond quickly. Approach them knowing that they are likely overworked and overwhelmed. Also, keep in mind that officials who are elected are often more willing to help citizens than are officials who are appointed. This is one reason why the state attorney general's office is a good place to go for help.

Non-Governmental Back-up

Two other good sources of help are state or national organizations. Some of these serve municipalities or municipal staff members. These include the National League of Cities, the U.S. Conference of Mayors, the International City/County Management Association, and the Government Finance Officers Association. Some of these also have chapters within states.

Other organizations such as the League of Women Voters and the National Taxpayers Union are designed to help ordinary citizens. In addition, there are numerous academic research centers that focus on public finance and budgeting such as the Tax Policy Center and the Tax Foundation. Many state universities also have local government research centers that focus on municipalities in that state. These are excellent, unbiased sources of help and information. On the Internet, one other excellent source of research on municipal issues is MuniNetGuide. Links to the Web sites of municipalities and organizations in each state can be found at another Web site, State and Local Governments on the Net (see Appendix).

A bit of searching will turn up all sorts of assistance for citizens who seek to be part of the local fiscal solution rather than part of the problem.

Appendix

Helpful Resources

Association of Local Government Auditors (www.governmentauditors.org)
449 Lewis Hargett Circle, Suite 290
Lexington, KY 40503-3590
859-276-0686

Governing Magazine **(www.governing.com)**
1100 Connecticut Ave. NW, Suite 1300
Washington, D.C. 20036
202-862-8802

Government Finance and Employment Manual, **U.S. Census Bureau (www.census.gov/govs/www/06classificationmanual/).**
U.S. Census Bureau
4600 Silver Hill road
Washington, D.C. 20233
800-923-8282

Government Finance Officers Association (www.gfoa.org)
203 N. LaSalle Street, Suite 2700
Chicago, IL 60601-1210
312-977-9700

Govmanagement.com (www.govmanagement.com)
P.O. Box 42264
Washington, D.C. 20015
202-239-6915

International Association of Assessing Officers (www.iaao.org)
314 West 10th Street
Kansas City, MO 64105
816-701-8100

International City/County Management Association (www.icma.org)
777 North Capitol Street NE, Suite 500
Washington, D.C. 20002-4201
202-289-ICMA

MuniNetGuide.com (www.muninetguide.com)
P.O. Box 533
Hinsdale, IL 60522-0533
847-337-3106

National Association of Counties (www.naco.org)
25 Massachusetts Avenue, NW
Washington, D.C. 20001
202-393-6226

National Association of Towns and Townships (www.natat.org)
1130 Connecticut Ave. NW, Suite 300
Washington, D.C. 20036
866-830-0008

National Civic League (www.ncl.org)
1889 York Street
Denver, CO 80206
303-571-4343

National League of Cities (www.nlc.org)
1301 Pennsylvania Avenue NW, Suite 550
Washington, D.C. 20004
202-626-3000

National League of Women Voters (www.lwv.org)
1730 M Street NW, Suite 1000
Washington, D.C. 20036-4508
202-429-1965

National Taxpayers Union (www.ntu.org)
108 North Alfred Street
Alexandria, VA 22314
703-683-5700

State and Local Government on the Net (www.statelocalgov.net)

Regionalism and Realism: A Study of Governments in the New York Metropolitan Area, Gerald Benjamin and Richard P. Nathan, Brookings Institution Press, 2001.

Tax Foundation (www.taxfoundation.org)
National Press Building
529 14th Street NW, Suite 420
Washington, D.C. 20045-1000
202-464-6200

Tax Policy Center (www.taxpolicycenter.org)
Urban Institute
2100 M Street NW
Washington, D.C. 20037
202-833-7200

U.S. Census Bureau, *Census of Governments* (www.census.gov/govs)
U.S. Census Bureau
4600 Silver Hill road
Washington, D.C. 20233
800-923-8282

U.S. Census Bureau, *Statistical Abstract* (www.census.gov/compendia/statab/)
See above address.

U.S. Conference of Mayors (www.usmayors.org)

1620 Eye Street NW
Washington, D.C. 20006
202-293-7330

Index

The Benefits of
AIER MEMBERSHIP

If you found this book helpful, you'll also benefit from AIER's newsletters. Our timely articles offer valuable insight on important economic and personal finance issues.

Our twice-monthly *Research Reports* provide concise discussion concerning a wide range of current issues. One article each month is devoted to deciphering where we are in the business cycle.

Our monthly *Economic Bulletin* presents in-depth treatment of topics pertaining to economics, fiscal policy, retirement, and personal finance.

Once you become a member you will also receive 50% off all AIER books. Support our educational efforts by becoming an AIER member today. Print and digital memberships now available.

Call us toll-free: (888) 528-1216

Visit us online: www.aier.org